attendance
Wesley Umi
Fall 1985

Candice Taite

887-4624

3810 S. Lindell

D1498557

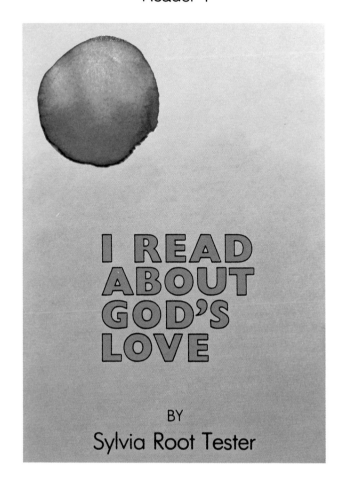

I READ ABOUT GOD'S LOVE

BY

Sylvia Root Tester

STANDARD PUBLISHING
Cincinnati, Ohio

2951

Illustrators:

Gwen Connelly, Pages 8-29, 32-39, 50-51, 57, 69, 75, 80-83, 112, 123
Frances Hook, Page 31
Dan Siculan, Pages 40-45, 109-111
James Seward, Pages 46-49, 52-56, 64-68, 76-79
Kathryn Hutton, Pages 58-62
Vera K. Gohman, Pages 70-74
Robert Masheris, Pages 85-89
Mary Ann Dorr, Pages 90-91
Mina Gow McLean, Pages 92-97
Helen Endres, Pages 98-103, 113-115, 119-121
Linda Hohag, Pages 104-107
Diana Magnuson, Pages 116-117

Cover Art by Nan Pollard

Unless otherwise noted, Scripture quotations are from
THE HOLY BIBLE: NEW INTERNATIONAL VERSION,
copyright © 1978 by the New York International Bible
Society. Used by permission.

Prepared for Standard Publishing by The Child's World.

ISBN 0-87239-661-4

© 1983. The STANDARD PUBLISHING Company, Cincinnati, Ohio.
A division of STANDEX INTERNATIONAL Corporation.
Printed in U.S.A.

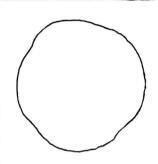

I READ
ABOUT
GOD'S
LOVE

TABLE OF CONTENTS

Stories

Poems, Prayers, and Puzzles

Bible Verses

Also in This Book

Introduction

Each child should learn to read the Bible for himself! This was an original intent of public school education. But today the Bible is seldom, if ever, mentioned in the public schools. Therefore, teaching a knowledge of God's Word is up to parents and Bible teachers. The Basic Bible Readers can help in the accomplishment of this goal.

While the readers probably will be used mostly in the home, they are valuable for Christian day schools and for the Bible school. And copies should be in every church library!

I Read About God's Love is the second in the Basic Bible Reader series. It is intended for the child who has almost completed the first grade.

Children may need help in decoding the new Bible-story words. Use the word lists in the back of the book for this purpose. Wherever possible, associate the words with pictures. This is extremely important in helping the child to understand what he is reading and to remember it.

From the wealth of Bible stories available, the contents of this and the other readers were selected for their appeal to the age group. Each book tells of Jesus so that the reader will begin to know and love Him and want to obey and follow Him. Old Testament stories are included in all but the Primer. They tell of worship, prayer, honesty, kindness, courage, and forgiveness. They encourage character development as they bring the reader closer to an understanding of the love of God.

Following A Tradition

The new Basic Bible Readers are a beautiful up-to-date edition of the famous Standard Bible Story Readers by Lillie A. Faris, that were first printed in 1925—and last revised in 1962. Millions of copies of these books have been added to the libraries of homes, schools, and churches.

The best of the former readers has been retained, including the favorite Bible stories that forever appeal to children. But the stories have been rewritten with a fresh up-to-date approach. And all of the illustrations are new—drawn by noted children's artists of today.

Whether it's a beginning reader with his very own primer, an older child enjoying his developing reading skills, or a parent, teacher, or grandparent, we think all will heartily agree: some traditions are worth preserving!

AWAY IN A MANGER

Away in a manger,
   No crib for a bed,
The little Lord Jesus
   Laid down His sweet head.

The stars in the sky
    Looked down where He lay,
The little Lord Jesus
    Asleep on the hay.

The cattle are lowing,
    The baby awakes,
But little Lord Jesus,
    No crying He makes.
I love Thee, Lord Jesus,
    Look down from the sky,
And stay by my bedside
    Till morning is nigh.

—Anonymous

IN BETHLEHEM

"We must go to Bethlehem," Joseph said.

"Why?" asked Mary.

"The ruler says we must.

We must go back to our home town.

We must sign up to pay taxes."

"Then let's get ready," said Mary.

"It will be hard for you," Joseph said.
"You are to have the baby soon."

"I'll be all right," Mary said.

Joseph and Mary left home.
Day after day they walked.
Sometimes Mary rode the little donkey.
Often they stopped, for Mary got tired.

One day they went up a hill.
Then they went up another hill.
And another.
Mary was very, very tired.
Soon they came to the top of another hill.

But many other people
had come to Bethlehem.

"There is no room here,"
said the man at the inn.
"No room at all."

Mary and Joseph turned to go.

"Wait!" called the man.
He looked at Mary.

He could see Mary was tired.
He could see Mary
was going to have a baby.

"I have a stable in back,"
said the man.
"You can stay in my stable.
It is warm in the stable."

"Thank you," said Joseph.
"Yes, thank you," said Mary.

Mary and Joseph went to the stable.
It was quiet in the stable.

And there in the stable,
baby Jesus was born.

Mary held baby Jesus.
"He is God's own Son," she said.

"Yes," said Joseph.
"He is God's own Son."

"Baby Jesus needs a bed," Mary said.

Joseph looked around.
He saw a manger.
He filled the manger with hay.

"Will this do?" Joseph asked.

"Yes," said Mary.
"It is a good bed."

Smiling, Mary laid the baby
in the manger.
There, among the animals,
baby Jesus went to sleep.

THE ANGEL'S GOOD NEWS

"Today . . . a Savior has been born to you; he is Christ the Lord."

—Luke 2:10, 11

It was night in Bethlehem town.

The little children were asleep.

The mothers and fathers were asleep.

Mary and Joseph were not asleep.

They were in the stable in back of the inn.

Mary and Joseph were looking
at the baby Jesus.

The baby Jesus was in the manger.

The baby Jesus was God's Son.

Out on a hill some shepherds
were watching their sheep.

The shepherds did not want
anything to hurt the sheep.

As they watched, they sat on the ground
and talked.

They watched the moon and stars.
Then something great happened.
The shepherds saw an angel.
The angel talked to the shepherds.

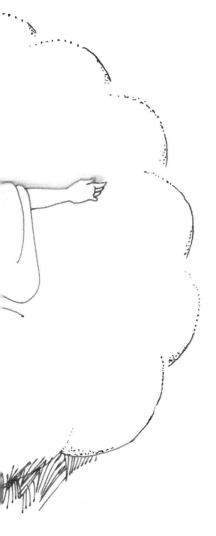

The angel said, "I bring you good news.
I have come to tell you that
Jesus is born.
You will find Him in Bethlehem.
You will find Him in a stable.
You will find Him in a manger."

Then more angels came.
More and more angels came.
The angels praised God.
Then the angels went away.

The shepherds said to each other,
"Let us go to Bethlehem
and see what has happened."

They went as fast as they could.
They did just what the angel
told them to do.
They went to the stable.
They found the baby Jesus.

The shepherds were glad.

They loved baby Jesus.

They said thank you to God
for sending His Son.
The shepherds said,
"We love You, baby Jesus.
We love You, God's own Son."

Mary Ann has learned the verses
that are on the next page.
She is thanking God for
sending the baby Jesus.
See if you can learn the verses.
Say them to your mom or dad.

THE SHEPHERDS

AND THE ANGEL

And there were shepherds living
out in the fields . . .
keeping watch . . . at night.
An angel of the Lord appeared
to them.
. . . the angel said . . .
"Do not be afraid.
I bring you good news
of great joy . . .
for all people.
Today in the town of David
a Savior has been born to you;
he is Christ the Lord."

—Luke 2:8-11

WHERE IS THE BABY KING?

Once there was a bright star.
It was brighter than the other stars.
It twinkled,
and it twinkled,
and it twinkled.

Some Wise-men were watching the sky.

They seemed to be looking for a new star.
They looked,
and they looked,
and they looked.
At last they saw the very bright star.

One Wise-man said,
"Look, there is a new star.
It must be the star
that tells us about the baby King."

The Wise-men were happy
and glad to see the new star.
The star seemed to say to them,
"Come with me.
I will show you
where to find baby Jesus."

The Wise-men got ready for the trip.
They said, "Let us take
some presents to the baby King."

One Wise-man took gold.

One Wise-man took frankincense.

Another Wise-man took myrrh.

The Wise-men got on their camels' backs.

The Wise-men rode a long, long way.

They watched the star.

It shone as brightly as it could.

It shone,

and it shone,

and it shone.

The Wise-men went to see King Herod.

They said, "Can you tell us where
to find the new baby King?"
King Herod's helpers said,
"He will be born in Bethlehem."

King Herod told the Wise-men this.
Then he said, "When you find Him,
come back.
I want to see the King too."

The Wise-men got on their camels.
The star went before them.
It stopped over the house in Bethlehem
where baby Jesus lived.

The Wise-men took their presents
into the house.
They gave the presents to Jesus.
"We love You, baby Jesus," they said.
They were very happy.
They had found the baby King.

WHAT CAN I GIVE HIM?

What can I give Him,
Poor as I am?
If I were a shepherd
I would bring a lamb;
If I were a wise man,
I would do my part—
Yet what can I give Him,
Give Him my heart.

—Christina G. Rossetti

31

JESUS IN DANGER

The shepherds were glad
when baby Jesus was born.
They went to see Him.

The Wise-men were glad too.
They took gifts to Him.

The bad King Herod was not glad.
He wanted to kill baby Jesus.
God said to the Wise-men,
"Do not go back to see the king.
He wants to kill baby Jesus.
Go home another way."

The Wise-men did as God said.

That night Joseph had a dream.
An angel said to him,
"King Herod will try to kill Jesus.
Take Mary and Jesus on a long trip.
Take them to Egypt.
I will tell you when to come back."

So, right then, Joseph got up.
He woke Mary.
"We must go," he said.
"We must go to Egypt."

Mary got up.

She put Jesus in a blanket.

She was careful not to wake Him.

"We are ready," she said.

Mary and Joseph and Jesus
left Bethlehem.

By morning, they were far from the town.

Day after day, they walked.

Sometimes Mary and baby Jesus
rode on a little donkey.

At last they came to Egypt.

"Here we are safe," said Mary.
"The bad King Herod cannot find us."

At last the bad king died.
The angel spoke to Joseph again.
"You can go back home now,"
the angel said.
"Jesus will be safe."

Joseph woke Mary and Jesus.
"Today is the day," he said.
"Today we start home."

Joseph and Mary were happy.
They were glad to take Jesus home again.

WHO AM I?

I brought messages from God.
I talked to Joseph.
I told him to go to Egypt.
Who am I?

I was outside at night.
I saw angels—many, many angels.
I worshiped baby Jesus.
Who am I?

I ruled a land.
I hated Jesus.
I wanted to kill Him.
Who am I?

I came from far away.
I saw a star.
I brought gifts to Jesus.
Who am I?

GOD'S PROMISES

Long before Jesus was born, God's helpers
told about Jesus' coming.
Here are some things they said.

*"The Lord your God
will raise up for you a prophet."*
— Deuteronomy 18:15

Jesus was that prophet.

"But you, Bethlehem . . .
though you are small . . .
out of you will come for me
one who will be ruler over Israel."

—Micah 5:2

Jesus was born in Bethlehem.

"For to us a child is born,
to us a son is given . . .
And he will be called
. . . Prince of Peace."

—Isaiah 9:6

Jesus is the Prince of Peace.

JESUS IN THE TEMPLE

As a boy, Jesus lived in Nazareth.
He grew and grew.
Soon He was twelve years old.

One day Joseph said,
"It is time for us to go to Jerusalem."

"Yes," said Mary.

Jerusalem was a big city.
Many people went to Jerusalem
at least once every year.
They worshiped God in the temple.

Soon the trip began.
All day, the people walked.
Day after day, they walked.
At last, they came to Jerusalem.

Joseph and Mary went to the temple.
Jesus went to the temple too.
They prayed.
They thanked God.
They told God they loved Him.

Then it was time to go home.
Mary and Joseph walked
with the others who were from Nazareth.
They walked all day.

Late in the day, they stopped.
Mary and Joseph thought Jesus
was with His friends.
But He was not.

"Where is Jesus?" Mary asked.
"I'll find Him," said Joseph.
Joseph looked and looked.
So did Mary.
But they could not find Jesus.

"We must go back to Jerusalem,"
Joseph said.

Joseph and Mary hurried back.
All the way,
they looked for Jesus.
But they didn't find Him.

Mary and Joseph went to the
place were they had stayed.
Jesus was not there.

They looked in the market place.
Jesus was not there.
They looked for three days!

At last, Mary and Joseph
went to the temple.
And there—there was Jesus!
But He was not alone.
All around Him were teachers.
Jesus listened to them.
He asked them hard questions.
And He answered *their* questions!
"How can One so young know so much?"
the teachers asked.

"Jesus!" Mary called.
"We were so worried about You!"

"You didn't need to worry," Jesus said.
"I'm doing the work of God,
my Father."

Then Jesus stood up.
He said good-by to the teachers.
He went home with Mary and Joseph.

The Bible says,
"Jesus grew in wisdom
and stature,
and in favor with
God and men."   —Luke 2:52

GOING TO THE TEMPLE

When people went to the temple, they sang this song.

I was glad when they said to me,
"Let us go into the house of the Lord."
I will now say,
"Peace be within you."
Because of the house
of the Lord our God
I will seek your good.

—*Psalm 122:1, 8, 9 New KJV*

A LITTLE SICK BOY

In a big city
lived an important man.
He was called a nobleman.
He had much money.
He had a big house.
Many people worked for him.
He had a little boy.
He loved his little boy very much.

One day the little boy got sick.
He got hot all over.
The boy's father was afraid—
afraid his little boy would die.

"We must find Jesus,"
the father said.
"He can make sick people well.
He can help my boy."

The father hurried to find Jesus.

"Jesus," he said.
"Please come to my house.
My little boy is very sick.
I know You can make him well."

Jesus smiled at the father.
"Go home," He said.
"Your son is well."

The man was so happy!
He started home right away.

The next day, as he was on his way home,
some men came running to meet him.

"Your little boy!" they said.
"He is better!
He is well again!"

"When did he get better?"
the man asked.

"Yesterday," said the men.
And they told him the time.

The man smiled.

"That's when I talked to Jesus," he said.

"I knew He could help me!"

The father hurried home.

He hugged his little boy.

Then he told his family about Jesus.

They all said, "Thank You, Jesus."

The father believed in Jesus.

The boy believed too.

So did all the other people in that house.

MORNING

The stars are gone,
The silver moon is hiding
from the sun.
A merry bird
just called to me,
"Wake up, the day's begun."
Good morning, world!
Good morning, God!

—Catherine Marshall

NIGHT

Tonight the earth
is crowned with stars,
a soft wind hums a tune,
And for a hat
the pine tree wears
a slice of saucy moon.
Good night, world!
Good night, God!

—Catherine Marshall

A LITTLE SICK GIRL

A little girl was sick,
very sick.
Her father, Jairus, was afraid,
afraid she might die.

The father ran to find Jesus.
There were many people around Jesus.

Jairus made his way through the crowd.
People saw him and moved out of the way.
Many knew Jairus.
He was a leader in his town.
People knew he was a good man.

"My little girl is dying,"
Jairus said to Jesus.
"Please come and touch her.
I know You can make her well."

"I will come," Jesus said.

But as they walked,
some people came to meet them.

"It is too late.
Your little girl is dead," they said to Jairus.
"There's no need to bother Jesus."

But Jesus said to Jairus,
"Don't be afraid. Believe in Me."

Jairus took Jesus to his house.
There, everyone was crying.

"There is no need to cry,"
Jesus told the people.
"The girl is not dead.
She is only sleeping."

Jairus took Jesus to the girl.
Jesus took her hand.
"Little girl," He said,
"Stand up."

The girl opened her eyes.
Then she stood up.

Jairus was so happy!
Jesus had made his little girl well!

"Give her some food," Jesus said.
"She is hungry."

Jairus did as Jesus said.
Then he turned to Jesus.
"Thank You," he said.
"Thank You for making her well."
We will always remember
Your goodness to us."

Jesus loves us.
Jesus is good to us.

What are some things
we can thank Him for?

JESUS LOVES THE LITTLE CHILDREN

"Jesus is coming," said the mothers.
They saw a crowd down the road.

"We want our children to see Jesus,"
said the mothers.
"Let's take them to Him."

"I hope Jesus will bless our children,"
said one mother.

"Yes," said another.

But when they got to where Jesus was,
they could not get close to Him.
The children could not even see Him.
Some tall men stood in their way.

"Jesus is busy," said one of the men.
"He doesn't have time for children!"

The mothers were sad.
So were the children.

Sadly, very sadly, they turned to leave.

But then Jesus said, "Wait. Don't go."
He said to His helpers,
"You should not have sent the children away.
Let them come close to me."

Jesus took the children in His arms.
He put His hands on their heads.
He held them close to Him.

"Jesus loves us.
Jesus loves us,"
the happy children said.
"We love Jesus too."

Jesus smiled at the children.
Then He said to the people,
"This is how to please God.
Become like these children."

THAT SWEET STORY OF OLD

I think when I read
That sweet story of old,
When Jesus was here among men,
How He called little children
As lambs to His fold,
I should like to have been with Him then.

I wish that His hands
Had been placed on my head;
That His arms had been thrown around me,
And that I might have seen
His kind look when He said,
"Let the little ones come unto me."

—Jemima Luke

ONE LITTLE LUNCH

"Mother," said the little boy.
"Jesus is not far from here.
May I go to see Him?"

"All right," she said.
"I'll make a lunch for you to take.
I'll give you five loaves of bread
and two fish."

The little boy took his basket lunch.
Off he went to see Jesus.

After a long walk,
he came to a big hill.
He saw Jesus.
Jesus sat on a rock.
His friends were near Him.
He was teaching.

There were many people on the hillside.
They were listening to Jesus.
The little boy
had never seen so many people!

The people stayed and stayed.
They listened and listened.
It got to be late in the day.

Then Jesus stopped teaching.
"Look at all these people,"
Jesus said to His helper, Philip.
"They are hungry.
Where can we buy food?"

The little boy looked at his lunch.
It was only five loaves of bread and two fish.
It was not much.
But he stood up.
Then he spoke to Andrew, one of Jesus' helpers.

"I have a little bit of food,"
he said. "If Jesus is hungry,
He can have it."

Andrew looked at the boy.
He smiled.

"You are a kind boy," he said.
"Let's talk to Jesus."

Jesus smiled at the boy.
He took the lunch from him.

"Ask all the people to sit down,"
Jesus said.
Then Jesus prayed.

The boy could hardly believe
what happened next.
Jesus broke the bread into pieces.
He gave the pieces to His helpers.
They gave them to the people.
Then there were not just a few pieces.
There were more and more!
And more!
Soon all the people had bread to eat.

Jesus did the same thing
with the two fish.
And all the people had fish to eat.

The people had all the food they wanted.
And there was food left over!

The little boy sat and ate.
"One little lunch," he said.
He shook his head.
"One little lunch!
And it fed all these people!"

A LITTLE SONG OF LIFE

Glad that I live am I;
That the sky is blue;
Glad for the country lanes,
And the fall of dew.

After the sun the rain;
After the rain the sun;
This is the way of life,
Till the work be done.

All that we need to do,
Be we low or high,
Is to see that we grow
Nearer the sky.

—Lizette Woodworth Reese

"There is nothing better for men
than to be happy
and do good while they live."

—Ecclesiastes 3:12

69

A LITTLE LOST LAMB

One day Jesus told this story:

Once there was a shepherd.
He had 100 sheep.
There were big sheep.
There were little sheep.
There were wee little baby lambs.
The shepherd loved his sheep.
He took good care of them.

Every day he led the sheep
to green grass.
Every day he led the sheep
to cold water.
Every night he counted the sheep
as he put them to bed.

One night the shepherd counted
only 99 sheep!
He counted them again!
There were only 99!
One little lamb was missing!

Darkness had come.
But the shepherd did not wait.
He hurried to look
for his little lost lamb.
He looked and looked.
He called and called.

At last, far, far away,
he heard a lamb's cry.
"Baa! Baa!"
It was a small, soft sound.

The shepherd hurried toward the sound.
And there—there was his little lost lamb.

"There you are!" said the shepherd.
He picked up the little lamb.
He carried him all the way home.

The shepherd was happy.
He had found his little lost lamb.

When Jesus finished the story,
He said,
"God is like the shepherd.
He is happy when someone who is lost
is found and brought back to Him."

JESUS LOVES YOU

As the Father has loved me,
so have I loved you.
Now, remain in my love. . . .

Love each other
as I have loved you. . . .
You are my friends
if you do what I command.

—John 15:9, 12, 14

PERFECT PRAISE

Jesus and His helpers
were on their way to Jerusalem.
Not far from Jerusalem was a small town.
Jesus told two of his helpers
to go into the town.

"You will find a donkey there," He said.
"Bring the donkey to me.
If someone asks you
why you are taking the donkey,
tell him that the Lord needs it."

The helpers hurried to the town.
They found the donkey
just as Jesus said they would.
They told the owners that
the Lord needed it.
They took the donkey to Jesus.

Some of the helpers put their coats
on the donkey's back.
Then Jesus got on the donkey.
Jesus rode the donkey
along the road to Jerusalem.

People put their coats
on the road in front of Jesus.
Some people waved palm branches.
As Jesus neared the big city,
someone shouted, "Jesus is coming!"

The news spread quickly.
Many people hurried to see Jesus.
Soon a great crowd gathered.

"Hosanna!" the people shouted.
"Jesus is our King!
He comes in the name of God!"
The people waved palm branches
as Jesus rode through Jerusalem.
Jesus stopped at the temple.
He got off the donkey and went in.

Children had followed Jesus
to the temple area.

They shouted praises to Jesus.
This made some men angry.
"Make those children stop," they said.

Jesus smiled at the children.
"The children give perfect praise,"
He said.

GATHER 'ROUND

Gather 'round, you children!
The King of glory comes.
Lay your branches in His way,
And praise His Holy Name!
Christ is coming! Join the chorus:
Lift your hearts and sing!
The King upon a donkey!
Let your loud hosannas ring!

—Mary Kay Bottens

A SONG OF PRAISE

All people that on earth do dwell
Sing to the Lord with cheerful voice;
Serve Him with joy, His praises tell;
Come now before Him and rejoice.

—William Kethe
adapted

Sing to the Lord

The American Indians had songs for everything that happened. Some Indians believed that at the time the earth was made, the Creator gave songs to the people. Some said that songs were given so that people could be "happy and enjoy themselves." They said, "The earth is alive, the dirt is alive. The songs . . . shake the earth."

"Shout for joy to the Lord,
    all the earth.
Let the sea resound,
    and everything in it,
the world,
    and all who live in it."

—Psalm 98:4, 7

NOAH'S BOAT

"Build a boat," God said to Noah.
"A great flood is coming.
It will cover all the earth."

Noah believed God.
He built the boat.
His sons helped him.

"Bring animals onto the boat,"
God said to Noah.
"Bring two of each kind.
A great flood is coming.
It will cover all the earth."

Noah believed God.
He found the animals, two of each kind.
And he brought them onto the boat.
His sons helped him.

"Take your family," God said to Noah.
"Take them onto the boat.
Take food with you.

A great flood is coming.
It will cover all the earth."

Noah believed God.
He took his family onto the boat.

Soon, rain poured down from the sky.
Water came up from under the earth.
For forty days, the rain fell.
For forty days and forty nights.

At last, the rain stopped.
"God has kept us safe," said Noah.

The waiting was not over, though.
The rain had stopped.
But the whole earth
was covered with water.

So Noah and his family waited.
Slowly, the water went down.
Months passed.

At last God said to Noah,
"You can leave the boat now."
So Noah, his family, and all the animals
left the boat.
Noah thanked God for keeping them safe.

Then God put a beautiful
rainbow in the sky.
"Whenever you see a rainbow," God said,
"it is My promise to you.
Never again, will there be a flood this bad."

And God has kept His promise.
Rains come. Even floods come.
But there has never been a
flood as bad as in Noah's day.

GOD'S RAINBOW

"I have set my rainbow
in the clouds...
Whenever I bring clouds
over the earth
and the rainbow
appears in the clouds,
I will remember my covenant*
between me and you
and all living creatures
of every kind.
Never again will the waters
become a flood
to destroy all life."

—Genesis 9:13-15

*"Covenant" means "promise."

POEMS FOR THE SEASONS

Wintry day! frosty day!
God a coat on all does lay.
On the earth, the snow He sheds,
O'er the lamb, the fleece He spreads,
Gives the bird a coat of feather
To protect it from the weather.

—unknown, adapted

The day before April
    Alone, alone,
I walked in the woods
    And sat on a stone.

I sat on a broad stone
    And sang to the birds.
The tune was God's making
    But I made the words.

—Mary Carolyn Davies

A bird's egg, a green branch,
A sweet, sweet tune,
A blue sky, a soft breeze —
That's June.

—Mary F. Butts

I like the fall,
The mist and all.
I like the night owl's
Lonely call—
And wailing sound
Of wind around.

—Dixie Willson

". . . in summer and in winter.
The Lord will be king
over the whole earth."

—Zechariah 14:8, 9

91

JOSEPH

Joseph was the son of Jacob.
Joseph had many big brothers.
But Joseph's father loved him best.

One day Joseph's father
gave him a gift.
It was a beautiful coat—
a coat with many colors!
Joseph liked his new coat.

But Joseph's brothers were jealous.
They knew their father loved Joseph best.
They began to hate Joseph.

Joseph's brothers were shepherds.
They took their sheep from place to place
to find grass.

One day Jacob said,
"Joseph, your brothers have been gone
a long time.
Go and find them.
Find out if there is trouble."

So Joseph went to find his brothers.
He walked and walked.

His brothers saw him coming.
"Look," said one brother.
"Here comes Joseph."
"Let's kill him," said another.

They didn't kill him.
But they took his coat of many colors.
And they threw him into a dry well.

Soon some people came by.
"We can make money," one brother said.
"Let's sell Joseph to these people."
So they did.
They sold Joseph as a slave.

Then the brothers went home.
They made Jacob believe that
a wild animal had killed Joseph.
Jacob cried and cried.
No one could comfort him.

But God took care of Joseph.
The people who bought Joseph
took him to Egypt.

One day, the king there
had a strange dream.
God helped Joseph tell the king
what the dream meant.

This made the king happy.
He made Joseph a ruler in Egypt.

While Joseph was ruler,
his brothers came to Egypt.
Their father sent them there to buy food.

When the brothers learned that Joseph
was a ruler in Egypt,
they were afraid!
But Joseph spoke gently to them.
"You meant to hurt me," he said.

"But God took care of me.
So don't be afraid.
I won't hurt you."

Joseph was kind to his brothers.
He sent food home with them.
Later the brothers came back
with their father.
Joseph was happy to see his father.
And Jacob was happy to see the son
he loved so much!

A LITTLE BASKET BOAT

One day, a baby boy was born.
He was a beautiful baby.
He was strong.
He was healthy.
His mother held him close.

"How can we keep our baby safe?"
the woman asked her husband.
"I don't know," he said.
"The king has said that all boy babies
of our people must be killed!"

"We will pray to God," she said.
"We will ask Him to help us."

The family hid their baby.
They hid him in a part of the house
where they thought he would not be found.
For three months, they kept him safe.

Then the baby got too big to hide.
His cries became stronger.
They knew someone would hear him.

"I have an idea," said the mother.
She found a large basket.
It was big enough to hold a baby.
And it had a lid.

She fixed the basket
so no water could get inside.
Then she placed the baby in the basket.
She walked down to the river.
The baby's sister, Miriam, went with her.
She placed the basket in the river
by some tall grass.

The basket floated like a little boat.
"He will be safe here," said the
mother to Miriam.
"But hide nearby and watch."

"Yes," said Miriam. "Don't worry, Mother.
I will watch our baby.
I will not let anything happen to him."

Soon, the king's daughter
and her helpers
came to the river.

The princess wanted to take a bath.
She waded out into the water.
"What's that over there?" she asked.
She had seen the basket boat.

"Get that and bring it to me," she said.
The maid brought the basket.
The princess opened the lid.
The baby was crying.

"Poor little baby," the princess said.
"You must be one of the babies
my father ordered killed."

The princess saw that this
was a very special baby.
"I won't let you be killed," she said.
"I'll take you to be my son."

Now Miriam ran up.
"I can find a nurse," she said,
"to take care of the baby for you."

"Yes," said the princess.
"Find a nurse."

Miriam ran home as fast as she could.
"Mother! Mother!" she called.
"Hurry! Come!"
She brought her mother to the princess.

"Here is your nurse," she said.

"Good," said the princess.
"Take this baby.
Take good care of him,
and I'll pay you well."

The mother took the baby into her arms.
She held his little body close against her.
How happy she was!

At home, the family took
good care of the baby.
They knew he was safe now.
He was the son of the princess!
Later he would go to live in the palace.
And he would be named Moses.
But for now, he was just their baby boy —
safe at home!

LOVE

by Jane Belk Moncure

What is love?

When your little brother is sick and can't play in
the snow, and you bring him a pan of snow, so he
can make a snowman—even a tiny one—that's
love.

Giving a friend a chance to jump rope once or
twice, that's love. *For love is kindness.*

Cutting a birthday cake so everyone has a slice, that's love. *For love is sharing.*

When your best friend can't have a birthday party because her dad is sick, and you take her a present anyway, that's love. *For love is caring.*

When Dad tells you to pick up your toys before watching TV, and you cheerfully obey, that's love. *For love is obeying.*

The Bible says,

"Let us love one another: for love is of God."
—1 John 4:7 KJV

Can you think of ways to show love for God?

SAMUEL, THE BOY HELPER

by Carol Ferntheil   revised and adapted

Hannah was very sad.
For many years, she had
wanted children.
But she had none.
One day, she went to God's house to pray.

"Please send me a son,"
she prayed to God.
"If You do, I'll give him back to You.
He can be a helper in Your house."

God heard Hannah's prayer.
He gave her a baby boy.
She named him Samuel.

Hannah took good care of her son.
She loved him very much.
She told him about God's house.
She told him of her promise.

When Samuel was old enough,
Hannah took him to God's house.
"I've come to keep my promise to God,"
she told the priest, Eli.
"This is my boy Samuel.
He will be a helper to you.
He is a good helper.
He will work hard."

Hannah was sad as she left her son.
But, as often as she could,
she came to see him.
And every year, she brought him a new coat.

One night, Eli had gone to bed.
Samuel was in bed too, in another room.
"Samuel," called a voice.
Samuel ran to Eli's room.
"Here I am," he said.
"I did not call you," Eli said.
"Go back to bed."

Samuel went back to bed.
Again the voice called, "Samuel!"
Again, the boy ran to Eli's room.
"I did not call you," Eli said.
Samuel went back to bed.

Then, a third time, the voice called.
A third time, the boy ran to Eli's room.
"The voice must be from God," Eli said.
"Go back to bed.

If the voice calls again, say
'Talk to me Lord; I will listen.' "

Once more, the voice called, "Samuel."
"Talk to me, Lord," the boy answered.
"I will listen."

And God talked to Samuel.
He told Samuel many things.
Samuel became a special helper of God's.

God talked to Samuel many times.
And Samuel always tried to do
what God wanted.

The Bible says,

*"The Lord was
with Samuel
as he grew up."*

—1 Samuel 3:19

A WORKER FOR THE LORD

I want to be a worker for the Lord.
I want to love and trust His holy Word.
I want to sing and pray
and be busy every day
In the work I do for the Lord.

—I. Baltzell, adapted

DAVID, A SHEPHERD BOY

by Carol Ferntheil
revised and adapted

David was a shepherd boy.
He took good care of his sheep.
He was very kind
to the little lambs.
Gently, he carried them
over the rough places.
He loved the sheep
and the little lambs.

In the morning, David would take
the sheep out in the fields.
He knew the sheep liked green grass.
Sometimes David would sing.
His voice was clear and soft.

Sometimes David would play his harp.
He made beautiful music.
Many of the songs in the Bible

are David's songs.
He wrote them.

One day, a big, old bear
ran after the sheep.
It grabbed a little lamb.
David was not afraid.
He chased the bear.

He took the lamb away from the bear.
He hit the bear and killed it!

"God helped me kill the bear," David said.
"The little lamb is safe.
God keeps me safe too."

Another day, a big lion came up.
David killed the lion too.
David was a good shepherd.
He loved and cared for his sheep.

SONGS OF DAVID

The Lord is my shepherd,
*   I shall lack nothing.*
*   He makes me lie down in green pastures,*
he leads me beside quiet waters,
*   he restores my soul.*

Surely goodness and love will follow me
*   all the days of my life,*
and I will dwell in the house of the Lord
*   forever.*
*   —Psalm 23:1-3, 6*

When I am afraid,
*   I will trust in you.*
*   In God, whose word I praise,*
*   in God I trust;*
*   I will not be afraid.*
*   —Psalm 56:3, 4*

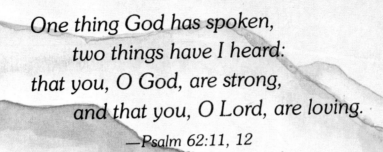

One thing God has spoken,
   two things have I heard:
that you, O God, are strong,
   and that you, O Lord, are loving.

       —Psalm 62:11, 12

The Lord is righteous in all his ways
   and loving toward all he has made.
The Lord is near
     to all who call on him,
   to all who call on him in truth.
The Lord watches over all who love him.

My mouth will speak in praise of the Lord.
   Let every creature praise his holy name
     for ever and ever.

      —Psalm 145:17, 18, 20, 21

DANIEL IN THE DEN OF LIONS

Once there was a little boy.
His name was Daniel.
His parents taught him to love God.
They taught him to pray to God.

One time soldiers came to Daniel's land.
They took many people away.
Daniel was taken far from home.

But still Daniel prayed to God every day.
He asked God to help him.
He tried not to be afraid.

Years passed.
Several kings ruled over the land
where Daniel was.
Each king knew that Daniel
was a good man who loved God.

When Darius became king,
he gave Daniel work to do.
The king knew that Daniel
would do what was right.

Some of the king's men
did not like Daniel.
They were jealous of him.

These men said, "Oh, King,
we need a new law.
Make a law that people
must pray only to you.
If anyone prays another way,
he will be put into a den of lions."

The king did what the men said.
He made the new law.
He did not know
that this would hurt Daniel.

But Daniel would not pray to the king.
He prayed to God.

Daniel prayed to God every morning.
He prayed at lunch time.
He prayed at night.

The king's men watched Daniel.
They saw him praying by his window.
They knew he was praying to God.
They saw that he prayed every day.

The men said to the king,
"Oh, King, Daniel is not keeping
your law. He is praying to his God."

The king was very sad.
"What have I done?" he said.
"I don't want to hurt Daniel."

"You must!" said the men.
"Even you, great King,
can not break your own law.
Throw Daniel to the lions!"

The king had to do as they wished.

So the men threw Daniel in the lions' den.
But God took care of Daniel.

In the morning the king went
to the lions' den.
He called, "Oh, Daniel, is your God
taking care of you?"

Daniel said, "God sent His angel
to keep me safe.
The lions have not hurt me."

The king was very happy.
"Daniel's God is real!" he said.
And from that time on,
he, too, prayed to God.

God sent an angel
to shut the lions' mouths.
The lions did not make a noise.
They did not open their mouths.

Thank You, Lord

Thank You, Lord, for loving me,
    caring for me,
    and helping me learn
    more about You.

Lead me, Lord,
    in the paths of Your love.

Help me to show Your love
    every day in all my work,
    in all my play,
    in what I do
    and what I say.

New Basic Bible Vocabulary

Of the words used in *I Read About God's Love*, 416 are words included on the *EDL Vocabulary List* or the *Macmillan Basic Vocabulary List* of first grade (or below) words or are words that were used in the Basic Bible Primer, *I Learn To Read About Jesus*.

The remaining 203 words are Bible words or words necessary to tell the Bible stories. These words are listed below.

Scripture quotations and poetry are exempt from vocabulary control.

11. often
pay
rode
ruler
taxes
12. rest
13. warm
14. held
15. among
hay
laid
17. asleep
18. happened
moon
19. happened
21. sending
24. bright
brighter
twinkled
25. bright
seemed
26. brightly
camels'
frankincense
myrrh
shone

28. camels
presents
32. kill
33. dream
Egypt
kill
34. blanket
careful
rode
wake
35. died
Egypt
spoke
36. brought
Egypt
messages
worshiped
37. brought
hated
kill
land
ruled
41. worshiped
43. answered
market
questions

young
44. worried
worry
47. important
Nobleman
48. meet
yesterday
49. hugged
knew
52. die
53. crowd
knew
leader
54. bother
dead
meet
touch
55. dead
56. goodness
remember
57. below
Bible
blind
crippled
deaf
healed

important
nobleman
59. busy
crowd
even
hope
60. held
61. become
65. hillside
listening
Philip
teaching
66. Andrew
cost
Philip
spoke
67. broke
few
happens
prayed
68. fed
shook
71. counted
led
wee
72. counted

darkness
73. Baa
    faint
    soft
    toward
74. brought
    carried
    finished
76. Lord
77. Lord
    owners
    rode
78. area
    branches
    crowd
    followed
    front
    gathered
    Hosanna
    palm
    quickly
    rode
    spread
    waved
79. angry
    perfect
    praises
84. brought
    build
    built
    cover
    earth
    flood
    Noah

86. cover
    earth
    flood
    forty
    kept
    Noah
    poured
    though
87. covered
    earth
    flood
    kept
    months
    Noah
    Noah's
    promise
    rainbow
    whole
92. Jacob
93. hate
    jealous
    knew
    trouble
94. dry
    grabbed
    Jacob
    kill
    killed
    sell
    slave
    threw
    wild
95. bought
    comfort

dream
Egypt
meant
strange
96. Egypt
    gently
    learned
    meant
    ruler
    spoke
97. Jacob
    later
98. babies
    healthy
    held
    husband
    killed
    strong
99. became
    enough
    idea
    kept
    large
    lid
    Miriam
    months
    river
    stronger
100. bath
    brought
    daughter
    floated
    happen
    lid

maid
Miriam
nearby
princess
river
waded
worry
101. killed
    Miriam
    nurse
    ordered
    poor
    princess
    special
102. against
    body
    brought
    held
    knew
    later
    Miriam
    Moses
    nurse
    palace
    pay
    princess
    safe
104. tiny
105. chance
    kindness
    twice
106. cheerfully
    obey
    obeying

       sharing
       slice
108. Hannah
       none
       prayed
       promise
       Samuel
       send
109. brought
       Eli
       enough
       Hannah
       often
       priest
       promise
       Samuel
       voice
110. Eli
       third
       voice

111. answered
       Bible
       Lord
       Samuel
       special
       voice
113. Bible
       carried
       clear
       David
       fields
       gently
       harp
       knew
       music
       rough
       soft
       voice
114. chased
       David's

       grabbed
       wrote
115. David
       hit
       kill
       killed
118. became
       Daniel
       Darius
       knew
       land
       parents
       prayed
       ruled
       several
       soldiers
       taken
       taught
119. anyone
       Daniel

       den
       jealous
       law
       prayed
120. Daniel
       done
       knew
       law
       prayed
       praying
121. Daniel
       den
       law
       mouths
       shut
       threw
       throw
122. Daniel
       den
       prayed

Cumulative Basic Bible Vocabulary

The following list includes all the words introduced as new Bible words or words necessary to tell the Bible stories in *both* the Basic Bible Primer and Basic Bible Reader, Grade One.

afraid	answered	bath	Bible
against	anyone	became	blanket
Amen	area	become	bless
among	arms	begged	blessed
Andrew	asleep	believe	blind
angels	Baa	below	body
angry	babies	Bethlehem	born

bother	dead	grabbed	kill
bought	deaf	Hannah	killed
branches	den	happen	kindness
bread	die	happened	knew
break	died	hardly	laid
bright	done	harp	land
brighter	donkey	hate	large
brightly	dream	hated	late
broke	dry	hay	later
brought	dying	healed	law
build	earth	healthy	leader
built	Egypt	held	learn
busy	Eli	helpers	learned
camels	enough	Herod	led
careful	faint	hillside	left
carpenter	fed	hit	lid
carried	few	holy	listened
chance	fields	hope	listening
chased	finished	Hosanna	loaves
cheerfully	floated	hugged	Lord
Christmas	flood	hundred	loving
clear	follow	hungry	maid
comfort	followed	husband	manger
cost	food	idea	market
counted	forty	important	Mary
counts	frankincense	inn	meant
cover	front	innkeeper	meet
crippled	full	Jacob	messages
crowd	gathered	Jairus	Miriam
Daniel	gently	jealous	months
Darius	gifts	Jerusalem	moon
darkness	God	Jesus	Moses
daughter	goes	Joseph	mouths
David	goodness	kept	music

myrrh	praying	shepherds	threw
Nazareth	presents	shone	through
nearby	priest	shook	throw
Noah	princess	shut	tiny
Nobleman	promise	sick	touch
none	questions	skip	toward
nurse	quickly	skipping	trouble
obey	rainbow	slave	true
obeying	remember	slice	twelve
often	rest	soft	twice
ordered	river	soldiers	twinkled
own	rode	son	voice
owners	rough	special	waded
palace	ruled	spoke	wake
palm	ruler	spread	warm
parents	safe	stable	waved
passed	Samuel	stood	wee
past	Savior	strange	week
pay	seemed	strong	whole
perfect	sell	stronger	wild
Philip	send	such	Wise-man
pieces	sending	taken	worried
poor	sent	taught	worry
poured	several	taxes	worshiped
praises	share	teaching	wrote
praised	shared	temple	yesterday
pray	sharing	third	young
prayed	sheepfold	though	